Calling

The shape had two heads ... *disappeared among the grave-stones, into the darkness.*

Joanne likes to read horror stories, and her favourite writer is Martin Wisemann. But the monsters from his stories are suddenly getting to be very *real*. Joanne knows there are monsters, but she also knows that you don't always *realise* they are monsters at first. Like the frightening Billy McGuire, who just didn't want to leave her.

Chris Westwood writes books for young people. For three years he worked for the music newspaper, *Record Mirror*, then he studied film and television at Bournemouth, on the south coast of England. He now lives in Pontefract, West Yorkshire.

The following titles are available at Levels 2, 3 and 4:

Level 2
The Birds
Chocky
The Canterville Ghost and the
    Model Millionaire
The Diary
Don't Look Behind You
Don't Look Now
Emily
The Fox
Flour Babies
The Ghost of Genny Castle
Grandad's Eleven
The Lady in the Lake
Money to Burn
Persuasion
The Railway Children
The Room in the Tower and Other
    Ghost Stories
Simply Suspense
Treasure Island
Under the Greenwood Tree
The Wave
We Are All Guilty
The Weirdo

Level 3
Black Beauty
The Black Cat and Other Stories
The Book of Heroic Failures
A Catskill Eagle
Channel Runner
The Darling Buds of May
Dubliners
Earthdark
Jane Eyre
Forrest Gump
The Fugitive
King Solomon's Mines
Madame Doubtfire
The Man with Two Shadows and
    Other Ghost Stories

More Heroic Failures
Mrs Dalloway
My Family and Other Animals
Not a Penny More, Not a Penny Less
Rain Man
The Reluctant Queen
Santorini
Sherlock Holmes and the Mystery
    of Boscombe Pool
StarGate
Summer of My German Soldier
The Thirty-nine Steps
Thunder Point
Time Bird
The Turn of the Screw
Twice Shy

Level 4
The Boys from Brazil
The Breathing Method
The Burden of Proof
The Client
The Danger
Detective Work
The Doll's House and Other Stories
Dracula
Far from the Madding Crowd
Farewell, My Lovely
Glitz
Gone with the Wind, Part 1
Gone with the Wind, Part 2
The House of Stairs
The Locked Room and Other
    Horror Stories
The Mill on the Floss
The Mosquito Coast
The Picture of Dorian Gray
Strangers on a Train
White Fang

For a complete list of the titles available in the Penguin Readers series please write to the following address for a catalogue: Penguin ELT Marketing Department, Penguin Books Ltd, 27 Wrights Lane, London W8 5TZ.

Calling All Monsters

CHRIS WESTWOOD

Level 3

Retold by John Escott
Series Editor: Derek Strange

PENGUIN BOOKS

PENGUIN BOOKS

Published by the Penguin Group
Penguin Books Ltd, 27 Wrights Lane, London W8 5TZ, England
Penguin Books USA Inc., 375 Hudson Street, New York, New York 10014, USA
Penguin Books Australia Ltd, Ringwood, Victoria, Australia
Penguin Books Canada Ltd, 10 Alcorn Avenue, Toronto, Ontario, Canada M4V 3B2
Penguin Books (NZ) Ltd, 182–190 Wairau Road, Auckland 10, New Zealand

Penguin Books Ltd, Registered Offices: Harmondsworth, Middlesex, England

First published by Viking 1990
This adaptation published by Penguin Books 1996
1 3 5 7 9 10 8 6 4 2

Illustrations by Rowan Clifford

Printed in England by Clays Ltd, St Ives plc
Set in 11/13 pt Lasercomp Bembo by
Datix International Limited, Bungay, Suffolk

To the teacher:

In addition to all the language forms of Level One and Two, which are used again at this level of the series, the main verb forms and tenses used at Level Three are:

- past continuous verbs, present perfect simple verbs, conditional clauses (using the 'first' or 'open future' conditional), question tags and further common phrasal verbs
- modal verbs: *have (got) to* and *don't have to* (to express obligation), *need to* and *needn't* (to express necessity), *could* and *was able to* (to describe past ability), *could* and *would* (in offers and polite requests for help), and *shall* (for future plans, offers and suggestions).

Also used are:

- relative pronouns: *who, that* and *which* (in defining clauses)
- conjunctions: *if* and *since* (for time or reason), *so that* (for purpose or result) and *while*
- indirect speech (questions)
- participle clauses.

Specific attention is paid to vocabulary development in the Vocabulary Work exercises at the end of the book. These exercises are aimed at training students to enlarge their vocabulary systematically through intelligent reading and effective use of a dictionary.

To the student:

Dictionary Words:

- When you read this book, you will find that some words are darker black than the others on the page. Look them up in your dictionary, if you do not already know them, or try to guess the meaning of the words first, without a dictionary.

Before you read:

1 *Calling All Monsters* is a **horror** story.

   a What other horror stories or horror films do you know the names of?

   b Which of them did you enjoy the most?

   c Why? Write a few lines about each of them.

2 Choose the *best* word or words to complete the sentence:

   a I saw a monster and it made me . . .

   cry   scream   wake up   laugh

   b He was not there, the house was . . .

   full   wet   empty   cold

   c It was . . . in the street, and I could not see.

   dry   full   funny   dark

   d I went to the . . . to buy some food.

   car park   cinema   supermarket   hotel

CHAPTER ONE

*Slowly, it began to move in the **grave**. The soft ground opened, and there was the moon in the sky.*

*It climbed up out of the darkness and saw grave-stones and trees, and a tall, locked **gate**. It heard a sudden noise, and ran to a tree.*

Just then, a light came on in a house across the street.

Joanne woke up hot and afraid, and switched on the light. A book of **horror** stories was on the table by her bed – *Dark Stories* by Martin Wisemann. 'I was reading it before I went to sleep,' she thought. 'Did it make me **dream**?'

Calmer now, she put out the light. There was a noise like a cat screaming, and she got out of bed and ran to the window. Nothing moved outside. Margaret, her older sister, lived down the road, and she had cats which she put out at night. 'Was that one of them?' Joanne thought.

One of the trees inside the **cemetery** was shaking now. Suddenly a bird flew out, and a shape dropped to the ground. Joanne's mouth opened in a silent scream. *The shape had two heads – and four arms and four legs!* It disappeared among the grave-stones, into the darkness.

A policeman was outside the front door when she came downstairs the next morning. He was talking to David.

'Something wrong?' she asked her mother in the kitchen.

'We'll know in a minute,' her mother said.

The front door closed and Joanne looked out of the window. The policeman was crossing the street. The cemetery gates were open, and two police cars were outside.

David came into the kitchen. 'Someone broke some grave-stones last night. They wanted to know if we saw anything.'

Joanne remembered the shape that came from the tree.

'Or was that part of my dream?' she thought.

David drove her to school. She still couldn't call him Dad. He

'Hallo, Jo,' he said. 'What are you doing tonight?'

was younger than her mother, and seemed more like an older brother than a father.

'Your last day,' he said. 'You have a week's holiday. What will you do? Hide in your room with your books?'

'If you really want to know, I've got some special English work to do,' she said. 'And I'll probably see Georgia.'

'And you'll see that boy of yours, Billy McGuire.'

Joanne didn't want to talk about Billy McGuire.

But she was worrying about him that evening when she saw him. She was in Malone's wine bar with Georgia and Georgia's new boy-friend, Tim. She meant to ask Georgia, 'What can I do about Billy?' but it was too late now.

'Hallo, Jo,' he said. 'What are you doing tonight?'

Joanne could already feel the evening going wrong. 'We're going to the cinema to see a film,' she said.

'Don't come if you don't want to,' Georgia said.

'I think I *will* come,' Billy said. He smiled.

'Why did I ever think I liked him?' Joanne thought.

Later, in the cinema, he put an arm round her shoulder, but she pushed it off. They were watching part of a film that was coming to the cinema the next week. It was called *The Slime*. Grey slime was getting into a house, and a man was screaming. The grey slime was moving towards him.

Billy was angry. 'What's wrong with you?' he said to Joanne in a loud voice. People turned to look at him.

'We need to talk,' Joanne said, softly.

'What about?' he said, loudly.

'I'll explain later,' Joanne said.

'Come on,' Billy said to her. 'If you've got something to tell me, you can tell me now.' He pulled her from the **seat**.

'Stop it!' Joanne cried.

'Joanne?' Georgia said.

'It's all right,' Joanne said quickly. 'You stay here.'

Billy pulled her out of the cinema, and into the street. 'You've got something to say to me,' he said. 'What is it?'

The shape moved fast and close to the ground, then it was gone. The car turned to miss it — and crashed into a wall.

Joanne couldn't look at him. 'Billy, I've tried to say this all week, but I wasn't sure –'

But something was happening in the road. A car tried to stop when a shape the size of a child ran in front of it. The shape moved fast and close to the ground, then it was gone. The car turned to miss it – and crashed into a wall.

'Stupid child!' someone said.

'*But it wasn't a child,*' Joanne thought.

She noticed a man in the street, and for a second or two he looked at her. '*He looks afraid!*' Joanne thought, before he turned and walked quickly away.

♦

Joanne was tired when she arrived home later. She wanted to sleep. 'But I must phone Billy first,' she thought.

'Did you have a good time?' her mother asked.

'It was OK,' Joanne said. 'Can I use the phone?'

'Yes, but don't talk too long,' her mother said. 'Your Uncle Ted is going to call. Mary is very ill and in hospital.'

'Oh dear!' Joanne said. 'I'll be as quick as I can.'

The phone was at the bottom of the stairs. While she waited for someone to answer at the other end, Joanne heard something move in the darkness between the stairs and the kitchen. But then Billy McGuire was saying, 'Hallo?'

'It's Joanne,' she said.

He was silent for a second, then he said, 'You didn't waste any time getting away after the accident, did you? Why are you calling? Just to say hallo?'

'To say goodbye, Billy.'

He was silent again. Then he said, 'What do you mean?'

'I mean that it's finished – you and me.'

'Why?' he said. 'Why are you doing this to me?'

'I'm sorry, Billy. It's best for both of us. I have to put the phone down now. There's nothing more to –'

'I loved you!' he said. 'Didn't you know –?'

Moonlight was shining across her little brother's face, so she closed the curtains before she went on to her room.

She put the phone down softly, her hand shaking. Then she heard something move again. But it was only the door to the **basement**. The phone rang, and Joanne picked it up, thinking it was about Mary. But it was Billy.

'You think I'm not good enough for you! Well, I'll show you how special I am!' And he put down the phone.

Joanne went upstairs, trying not to think about him. She looked into Jason and Sarah's room. Moonlight was shining across her little brother's face, so she closed the **curtains** before she went on to her room.

She had lots of books, and many were horror stories. She liked Martin Wisemann's books. There was one about a thing that climbed up out of a grave. She found it – and saw a photograph of Martin Wisemann on the back.

She remembered the face in the crowd at the accident.

It was the same face.

CHAPTER TWO

It was Saturday morning, and Joanne sat in the kitchen drinking tea. Sarah, her nine-year-old sister, came in.

'Are you going to town to see that boy?' Sarah asked her. 'I don't like him.'

'No, I'm not seeing him any more,' Joanne said.

'Good,' Sarah said. 'Do you ever have strange dreams? I had one last night, and you were in it. You came into my room while I was asleep, and you shut the curtains.'

'That wasn't a dream. I did come into your room.'

Sarah shook her head. 'There was a monster waiting in the dark, but there was just enough light to stop it doing anything. Then you came and took the light away, and I heard the monster get ready to come out.'

'And did it?' Joanne said.

'No, because, in the dream, I woke up. I ran and opened the

curtains, and the light came in. The monster was in the garden, looking up at my window, but it ran away.'

'There are no monsters,' Joanne said. 'Only in books.'

But later, on the bus, Joanne decided that there *were* monsters, but you didn't always realise that's what they were at first. Her real father died when she was eleven, and that was the first time she knew about real monsters, and the terrible things they could do.

The bus stopped in Ashbourne Road, and Billy McGuire was waiting. He got on and went upstairs without seeing her.

They went past the top of a narrow road which went down to Westbury – a group of pretty little houses. Joanne and her father always wanted to live down there, but the monsters took him away before that could happen.

She got off the bus before it got to the town. But when it moved away, Billy looked down and saw her in the street. He was angry, and said something which she couldn't hear.

Joanne ran down a narrow street, and hurried towards Carleton's Bookshop. She went up the stairs to a room full of old books, but she went straight to the window. Five minutes later she heard someone come into the shop, then heard the customer talking to Mr Carleton. It was a man's voice, but it wasn't Billy's.

After another five minutes, Joanne decided that it was safe to go. The man was leaving with a bag full of books when she got downstairs. It was Martin Wisemann.

Joanne wanted to say something, but he was almost out of the shop door. At last she found her voice. 'Martin, is that you?'

He stopped outside and looked at her. 'Have we met before?'

'I saw you at the accident last night. I thought you noticed me, but I wasn't sure.'

'Oh, *that*. Yes, I remember.'

'You left very quickly.'

'Yes . . .' he said. 'I always *want* to stand and look, but I don't like doing it. Who are you?'

He stopped outside and looked at her. 'Have we met before?'

'Joanne Towne,' she told him.

'Was there something you wanted to talk to me about?'

What *did* she want to say? 'I've read most of your books,' she said. 'I think you're the best.'

'Listen, I'm in a bit of a hurry. Can we walk? My car's just round the corner.'

She had to run to stay with him. 'Are you writing another book? It's been ten years since your last one.'

'I still write, but only for myself now.' He saw that she didn't understand this. 'It would take too long to explain,' he said. They were at his car now, and he unlocked the door and jumped in.

'I think you can help me with my special English work,' she said. 'I could write about your books, and about you.' He didn't look happy. 'Will you think about it? Please?'

He looked closely at her for several seconds, then he said, 'Come to my house and we'll talk about it. I live about a mile and a half south of the town. There's a road that goes down through some trees —'

'Westbury,' Joanne said.

'You know it?'

'I dreamed about living there when I was younger,' she said.

'Come when you can, and we'll talk,' he said. He looked at his watch. 'Now, I have to go.'

'Yes, of course. Thank you,' she said.

But he was already driving away.

◆

Joanne met Georgia a bit later and they ate at Pizza-Face. There was a large smiling 'face' of a pizza painted on the wall. Joanne didn't like the face, and she turned away from it before she told Georgia about Martin Wisemann. Then she explained about Billy. 'I can't forget his angry face on the bus today,' she said. 'It frightened me.'

'Forget about him. Come to Hazel's party tonight. Her parents are away, and there will be lots of boys there!'

There was a large smiling 'face' of a pizza painted on the wall.
Joanne didn't like the face . . .

Joanne smiled. 'OK, I'll come.'

It was four o'clock when she thought about Martin Wisemann again. She was going home on the bus and saw a man reading a local newspaper. There was a report on the front page about the broken grave-stones in the cemetery.

Joanne remembered her dream. Perhaps she could tell Martin about the shape from the tree. Wasn't it like something in one of his books? She remembered his frightened face at the accident. Could she ask him about that, too? She looked out and saw that they were near Westbury. 'Why don't I go and see him now?' she thought.

She got off the bus and walked through the trees to the houses. One stood away from all the others. She didn't *know*, but she was sure it was Martin's. There was no car outside, and she went round to the back door – and was surprised to find it unlocked. After a minute, she went in.

She walked through the kitchen to the living-room. There were lots of books on **shelves** round the walls, and a photograph of a woman about thirty years old, on a table.

Joanne went into the other downstairs room. There were papers everywhere – on a desk, on chairs, on the floor. Most were half-finished stories. And there was the bag of books from the bookshop. She looked and was surprised to see that every book inside it was a Martin Wisemann book.

There was a box of thrown-away pages of stories by the desk, and she saw that one was called *Cereal Killer*. After a second, she put some pages into her pocket.

Suddenly there were noises above her head. Was Martin upstairs? No, his car wasn't here. Perhaps he had a cat or dog. But why keep it upstairs? She hurried back towards the kitchen – and heard a cry. She looked up and saw a closed door at the top of the stairs. *And something was trying to open it.*

Joanne ran from the house and did not turn round until she was at the garden gate. She looked back and saw that some of the upstairs windows had wood over them.

12

CHAPTER THREE

Tim was one of only four boys at Hazel's party.

'Georgia says you saw Martin Wisemann today,' he said.

'That's right,' Joanne said. 'He was buying all the Martin Wisemann books in Carleton's Bookshop.'

Tim said, 'That's strange. I thought I saw him in two other bookshops last week. Does he live near here?'

'In Westbury. I – I'm going there to meet him soon. I want him to help me with my special English work. I want to write something about him and his books.'

She heard several male voices all talking at once. Then from somewhere near her she heard Georgia say, 'Oh, no!' She looked round and saw Billy McGuire and two of his friends. Billy was looking at Joanne and Tim.

'We have to talk,' Billy told her. 'Is this your new boyfriend? Does he know about the old man you tried to be friendly with outside the bookshop? Oh, yes, *I* saw you!'

'Tim's just a friend,' Joanne said. She turned away, but Billy held her arm.

'I haven't finished with you yet,' he said.

'Take you hands off me, or I'll –'

'What?' Billy said, smiling. 'What will you do?'

'Just take your hands off her,' Tim said.

The room was suddenly silent. Joanne said, 'Don't say any more, Tim.' To Billy she said, 'Let go of my arm or someone will phone the police.' Someone was already on the phone. She saw Georgia speaking into it across the room.

Tim threw himself at Billy and pulled Joanne free. Billy fell against the wall.

'You go,' Tim told Joanne. 'I'll follow you.'

But the next second Billy pushed him down to the floor and went after Joanne.

She ran into the street, then stopped and looked back. There

13

were some shouts and the sound of breaking glass, then five or six people came out of the house.

'Move!' someone screamed at her. It was Georgia. Tim was just behind her. They went the wrong way for Joanne's home, so she ran the opposite way. Billy ran after Joanne, and his friends went after Tim and Georgia. She took a quick look back – and fell over. When she looked up, Billy was standing over her.

'Billy, can we please talk about this tomorrow? I –'

'No,' he said, angrily. 'You said you loved me, but it was a *lie*.' He moved towards her. 'Now I'm going to –'

Suddenly, she heard and saw something behind him. And then *he* was screaming ... '*I've read this before!*' she thought, wildly. Then she remembered! 'This happened in *Night Walk*, one of Martin Wisemann's stories! Oh, no! Maybe it's only a dream!'

Surely only a dream could explain the tree that was moving through the darkness. But it wasn't a *tree*! Its left arm was holding Billy McGuire round the throat. And the right hand was holding a knife.

Joanne turned and ran.

♦

She couldn't sleep. She lay in her bed thinking. 'Why didn't I stay and help Billy?' But she knew the answer: she didn't want to die too. 'Did somebody read *Night Walk*, and then steal the idea and . . . *do* it?'

It didn't explain the frightened look on Martin's face at the accident. Or the books from Carleton's Bookshop. And what about the noises upstairs in his house?

Joanne remembered the pages from Martin's work-room. 'Perhaps they'll help me to understand,' she thought.

She got out of bed and took the pages to the kitchen. Then she made a cup of coffee and began to read.

They were just stories, that was all. *Cereal Killer* was about

Its left arm was holding Billy McGuire round the throat. And the right hand was holding a knife.

the Honey Monster who escaped from its cereal box and then bit the heads off three children. The next few pages were from a story about a girl fighting something locked in the basement and which was pushing against the door. Another page was about something happening in a cinema.

A car stopped outside the house, and Joanne found herself going to open the front door – like a girl in a story, but she didn't know which one.

A policeman and policewoman were outside.

'Do you know Billy McGuire?' said the policewoman.

CHAPTER FOUR

She tried not to think about Billy McGuire. Each time she met Georgia and Tim in the wine bar, they said nothing about it. At night she wanted to read, but she was too afraid. The holiday week was going quickly, and she still had to start her special English work. Then, on Thursday morning, she looked out of her bedroom window at the cemetery and looked at Billy McGuire's new grave.

The bedroom door opened behind her.

'Jo?' It was Georgia. 'Your Mum told me to come up.'

'I was just looking at –' Joanne began.

'Yes, I can see,' Georgia said.

'I want to explain things to Billy's parents,' Joanne said. 'But what can I say to them? Billy only died because he followed me.'

'Don't *think* like that,' Georgia said. 'Billy came to the party looking for trouble. Everyone saw that, and they told the police. Now they're looking for his killer.'

A bit later they went to the park and sat near the lake.

'What about your English?' Georgia said. 'I thought Martin Wisemann asked you to go and see him.'

'He did,' Joanne said.

16

'So stop feeling sorry for yourself. Go and see him!'

'OK,' Joanne said after some minutes. 'I'll go back there as soon as I can.'

'Go *back*? Have you been there already?'

Joanne found that she wanted to tell Georgia everything.

Georgia listened silently, then said, 'What do you think Martin Wisemann keeps upstairs in his house?'

'I'm only telling you what I *thought* I heard,' Joanne said. 'But there have been other things.'

'What other things?'

'Remember the accident outside the cinema last week? I'm sure it wasn't a child or an animal that ran in front of that car.'

'Did any other person –?' Georgia began.

'Martin was there. I didn't ask him if he saw it.'

Georgia thought for a minute, then said, 'Wisemann is behind all this. And then there's you.'

'And I'm afraid,' Joanne said.

◆

There was bad news when Joanne got home from the park.

'Uncle Ted phoned,' Joanne's mother told her. 'Mary is very, very ill now. David is going to drive me to see her. We'll probably have to stay for two or three days.'

'I'll look after Jason and Sarah,' Joanne said.

'We'll be back by Sunday,' David said. And late that evening, after Joanne locked all the doors and windows, David phoned to say that they were safely in Wolverhampton.

Next morning, Joanne phoned Martin's number, but there was no reply. 'I've got to see him,' she thought.

'I have to go to the supermarket,' she told Sarah.

'OK,' Sarah said.

'Only answer the door if you know who it is,' Joanne said. She heard a noise coming from between the stairs and the kitchen. 'And shut that basement door. If Jason–'

'OK, OK! Just go to the supermarket!' Sarah told her.

Joanne went to the nearest supermarket. She pushed a **trolley** between the shelves of food, and began to put things in it.

'I'll have to take all this home before I can go to Martin's,' she thought, and put a pizza into the trolley.

She was picking up a packet of chocolate cakes when she heard a loud crash to her right. A woman was sitting on the floor holding a packet of Honey Cereal. A shape disappeared round the corner of the shelves.

Joanne left her trolley and ran towards the woman. 'Is there anything –' She stopped. *There was a hole in the cereal box instead of a picture of the 'Honey Monster'.*

Now there was another crash, then another. Joanne ran round the corner. There were boxes and tins of food all over the floor.

And at the end of the shelves stood the Honey Monster.

He was seven feet tall. 'Joanne,' he said.

He knew her name.

'Who told you my name?' she said.

'Don't you know who I am, Mummy?'

'I'm not your mummy!' She picked up a bottle and threw it. It fell and broke in front of him. 'Go away!' she shouted. 'Help! Help!' She threw another bottle, and it broke against the Honey Monster's face.

He pushed some shelves over. 'I'll get you for this!' he shouted. 'You and the person who brought me here!' And he began to climb up the shelves towards the ceiling.

'What do you mean?' she said. 'Who *did* bring you here?'

But the Honey Monster made a hole in the ceiling and climbed into the darkness above, then disappeared.

The supermarket manager was coming towards her now. 'What happened?' he was saying. 'Who was it? Did you see who did all this? Can you describe them?'

'I –' Joanne shook her head. 'It all happened too quickly,' she said weakly. And she found her trolley and got out of the supermarket as quickly as she could.

She was sure that the Honey Monster was part of Martin

She threw another bottle, and it broke against the
Honey Monster's face.

Wisemann's story, *Cereal Killer*. 'I was wrong to leave Jason and Sarah alone,' she thought.

And she began to run.

♦

Jason was watching a horror film on TV. Joanne quickly turned it off. 'Why did you –?' she shouted at Sarah.

'I couldn't find another film,' Sarah said. 'What's the matter with you?'

Joanne tried to calm herself. 'I'm sorry. Can you bring in the shopping bags?' While Sarah did this, she tried to phone Martin, but there was still no answer. She went to the basement, opened the door and switched on the light. There were no monsters. She shut the door again, then went into the kitchen to put the shopping away.

Two minutes later, the phone rang. It was Martin.

'Joanne Towne?' he said. 'We met at the bookshop.'

'I planned to come and see you,' Joanne said.

'Come as soon as you can,' he said.

'Is something wrong? Martin, I don't understand –'

'There isn't much time. Get over here as quickly as you can, and be careful. Are there others in your house?'

'Yes,' she said.

'Take them somewhere safe. I can't explain now –'

There was a scream, and Joanne dropped the phone and ran to the kitchen. Sarah was holding Jason, and shaking. Joanne looked at the table . . . and wanted to scream, too.

Pizza-Face was moving across it.

'Jo!' Sarah cried. 'What *is* it?'

'I – I don't know,' Joanne said. But she *did* know. It was another idea from a Martin Wisemann story. 'I remember reading it,' she thought, 'and now it's **come alive**!'

She ran to a cupboard and took out the biggest knife she could find. The pizza was getting ready to jump. When it did, Joanne cut it in half. But now there were *two* pizzas moving

20

Sarah was holding Jason, and shaking. Joanne looked at the table . . .
and wanted to scream, too. Pizza-Face was moving across it.

across the table! Joanne brought the knife down again and again. Smaller pizzas jumped off the table and ran across the kitchen floor.

'Help!' Sarah screamed.

Joanne saw the **vacuum cleaner** in the corner of the room. She got it, and switched it on. 'Take Jason to Margaret's house and stay there until I come for you!' she shouted at Sarah.

Sarah took Jason and ran from the house. Joanne began to clean up the little pizzas with the vacuum cleaner. Soon it was full, and it shook and jumped all over the floor. Joanne dropped the vacuum cleaner, *but it came after her!*

She ran out of the kitchen and started to turn to the front door, but she stopped suddenly by the basement door. The vacuum cleaner came towards her, smoke coming from it. She kicked open the basement door, took the vacuum cleaner with both hands, and threw it down the stairs.

She heard it crash at the bottom, then she pushed the door shut. After a minute, something came up the stairs and pushed against it, but didn't open it. 'Perhaps it has no hands!' Joanne thought wildly.

She looked at the front door and saw that it was open wide. *And there, fresh from the grave, was Billy McGuire.*

CHAPTER FIVE

'I haven't finished with you yet,' he said.

'B—but you're dead,' she said.

'And you killed me,' he said. 'You took away everything I had, and I died because of you.'

'No! That's not true, Billy,' Joanne said.

A sound came from the basement. Billy did not seem to notice. There was a wild look in his eyes. He wanted her to go to the grave with him. She ran upstairs to the bathroom, and locked the door behind her. A second later he was knocking and kicking it.

The vacuum cleaner came towards her, smoke coming from it.

Joanne pulled herself away from Billy, and Martin took a gun from his jacket pocket. 'Go to the car!' he shouted.

'Open this door!' he shouted. 'I love you. I want us to be together always.'

She ran to the window and looked out. A car stopped outside, and Martin Wisemann got out. Joanne opened the window. 'Martin! Help me! Be careful, but help me!'

Martin walked calmly but quickly towards the front door. Then the bathroom door crashed open and Billy was coming towards her. She threw herself wildly to the left, but Billy held her arm. They were half out of the bathroom, and now Martin was at the top of the stairs. He saw Billy and a look of horror came to his face.

Joanne pulled herself away from Billy, and Martin took a gun from his jacket pocket. 'Go to the car!' he shouted.

She half-fell down the stairs. There was the sound of the gun – and everything was silent for a minute. Then she heard Martin say, 'How could I be so –'

She couldn't hear the rest of his words because of the noise from the basement. Something was kicking the door again. Then Martin was running downstairs, the gun in his hand and his mouth wide open. Billy was behind him.

Martin pulled her into the car, and she looked back at the house. There was no Billy. She thought she saw the basement door open, but nothing came out of it. Martin threw the gun into the back of the car, then drove away.

'Martin, you have to tell me what's happening.'

'Yes, I know that now,' he said. 'But I had to be sure that it was you I was looking for.'

'*You* were looking for *me*?'

'Yes. After we met last week, I decided to call you later that day, but you were out. Then there was a report of Billy McGuire's killing in the newspaper, and your name was there.' He looked at her. 'It was *Night Walk*, you probably realised that.'

'Were you looking for me *before* you met me?' she said, suddenly beginning to understand.

25

*Joanne almost screamed. A blue-grey slime was over all the grass,
and the garden chairs.*

'Yes, and you were looking for me. You were looking for an escape from your boring world, and you chose me and my stories. I'm like you. Why do you think I have to write these stories, when nobody reads them any more? Because I want the excitement. But it's my plan to make everyone safe that matters now.'

She looked at him. 'Martin, are you telling me that you *made* those – those horrors come alive?'

'Yes,' Martin said. 'But so did you.'

They were driving through the open gates outside Martin's house . . . and Joanne almost screamed. A blue-grey slime was over all the grass, and the garden chairs.

'It started days ago,' Martin told her.

He parked near the front of the house and they walked round to the back. Joanne saw more of the slime there.

'What is it?' she asked.

'A warning,' he said. 'To tell us that it's all coming to an end.' He unlocked the back door and they went through to the living-room. 'Sit down and be comfortable.'

She sat in a chair near the fire and picked up the photograph on the table. 'Your wife?' she said.

'Yes. She died ten years ago. Her name was Josie, and I loved her more than I can say. I was always afraid something would happen to her, and I tried to write about it. I always do that with the things that frighten me. I wrote a story about the thing I was afraid of most – Josie dying. I felt better then. There was no need to feel afraid, I told myself. The worst was finished, but it was only a story.

'But then she died in an accident. *The same accident that I wrote about in the story.* I – I killed her. Somewhere between me writing it and Josie reading it –' His voice was shaking. 'Do you begin to understand?'

'But it *was* only a story,' Joanne said.

'Do you feel like that when you read a good book? When you lose yourself in a story and don't want to go back to the real world? Do you feel it's only a story then?'

27

He took one of his books from a shelf and threw it on the fire, and they watched it burn.

'No,' Joanne agreed. 'No, I don't.'

'They're just words on a page to some people. But we escape to another world. Between us, because of us, something comes alive that wasn't alive before. But there was something more that I didn't realise until I lost Josie.'

'What was that?' Joanne was almost afraid to ask.

'We make monsters come alive too.'

Don't let it be true, she thought.

'There were no more books after Josie died,' he went on after a minute. 'I have to stop them going out into the world and making more monsters. But there are books on every shelf in every bookshop. So now I move to other towns to try and forget. Then someone like you gets near me, and things begin to happen. But you're not the first.' He took one of his books from a shelf and threw it on the fire, and they watched it burn.

'You came to Westbury and found me, and saw that something was wrong,' she said. 'Now you're buying all your books to stop me reading them. But what about the monsters that are *already* alive because of us?'

There was a noise, and he looked up at the ceiling.

'Are some of them in the house?' she asked.

'Yes. But as long as they're here it's all right.'

She jumped up out of the chair. 'I want to see them.'

'Haven't you seen enough?' But he took her upstairs to the bathroom. In the centre of one wall was a small hole.

'Look through there,' he said.

At first she saw only darkness, but then she saw grey-white shapes. Some were asleep on the floor, others moved across the room . . . and they had no faces. 'I saw one of these before,' she thought. 'It ran out in front of the car outside the cinema.'

'Now you've seen everything,' he said quietly.

'But, Martin, they're not —'

'Finished? That's right. They're ideas waiting to be finished. Stories, monsters, people that want to come alive. I can't stop ideas coming. I can't stop myself thinking, that's the problem.

29

The ones making the noise are the worst. They're the stories I'm writing now, or I'm thinking of writing. But if anyone ever reads them . . .'

Joanne understood now. 'I read *Cereal Killer* and because I **believed** that the Honey Monster was real, it came alive,' she thought.

'But what are we going to do with them?' she said. 'You can't just leave them there.'

'No, I can't,' he said.

CHAPTER SIX

He took her to his work-room. 'I want you to read my new book,' he said. And he gave her some pages of writing.

'I thought you were burning all your books,' she said.

'This is different. Read it, and you'll understand.'

And while Martin sat and smoked cigarettes, Joanne read the pages of writing. Most of the story was about herself. She could almost taste and touch the things in it. But then the book ended, just when she wanted to know more.

'You're the man in the story,' she said. 'You're the writer and the man who makes monsters. The girl is me. But you haven't finished it.'

'I need your help to do that. I'll write the end – and you'll live it. This is what you have to do . . .'

♦

It was dark when he walked out to the car with her. He started it, then held the door open for her.

'Can you drive?' he asked.

'I can make it go or stop. It's enough.'

She waited for him to go back and start writing again, then she drove away from the house. She could see the blue-grey slime on the grass, and a piece the size of a man got on to the

While Martin sat and smoked cigarettes, Joanne read the pages of writing.

She could feel Martin writing about her, and the things she was doing.

car. It got half-way through her open window, and it smelled like bad food. She went faster and pulled the car very near to a tree. Her unwanted passenger hit the tree and fell off. Then she shut the window.

'Stay calm,' she told herself, and drove on.

There was something in front of her. It was Billy's killer, from *Night Walk*! Joanne drove towards it and closed her eyes. Again there was the smell of bad food, but nothing to stop her.

She could feel Martin writing about her, and the things she was doing. There were noises coming from the fields, like the cries from the cemetery but much louder. 'It's all part of Martin's story,' she told herself.

She could see the lights of the town now. Then something came up out of the river at the side of the road. She saw its eyes, and smelled the bad smell. Suddenly everything went black, and Joanne stopped the car. The THING was all over the car windows, and she could see a face with a hundred eyes looking at her.

She remembered the gun in the back of the car. Did he tell her about the gun? Was it in the story? It didn't matter, it was all she had. She picked it up and shot the THING. The glass in the car window broke into a thousand pieces – and so did the THING.

Joanne drove on. The crowd of shapes following her got bigger. Half a mile from the town, the car stopped and wouldn't start again. Every horror story had a closed door or a car that wouldn't start, Joanne remembered. She got out and began to run. She heard feet behind her. She ran as fast as she could, and probably as fast as Martin could write the words that described the narrow streets, or the monsters following her. The town was empty. The shops were closed. She saw dark shapes coming from shop doorways. But where did Martin want her to go now?

Then she saw the cinema, and she ran inside.

It was only when she sat in a seat that she realised the cinema was empty. A film was showing. A man was locking the doors

A scream made her turn back, and the man in the film was screaming because slime was coming into the bathroom.

and windows of his house. He went into the bathroom to shave. Joanne looked round the cinema. Here and there were dark shapes. A scream made her turn back, and the man in the film was screaming because the slime was coming into the bathroom. Joanne looked across the seats in the cinema, but couldn't see anything because it was getting darker and darker. Now the man was running from his bathroom and down the stairs. Everywhere he went there was more grey slime. Then several shapes that were not in the film came flying towards Joanne out of the dark.

She closed her eyes. 'If I open them now,' she thought, 'I'll look into the face of something that will kill me.'

'Joanne,' a voice said softly.

They knew her name. She put her hands over her face. 'It will finish as soon as Martin writes the end of the story,' she thought.

'Joanne,' the voice came again.

It was followed by a crash of furniture, and a long scream. Joanne pushed her hands closer to her face and over her eyes. Inside her head she could see it all. Grey slime was coming out of the film and into the cinema. She could see it begin to eat the dark shapes, one after another. Soon there were only a few of them left, and they were not dangerous. Martin was winning. 'Martin wanted them to follow me,' she thought. 'Now it's finished.' ·

She opened her eyes . . .

And saw the shapes above her. Shapes that were holding out their hands and saying her name.

'Joanne, come with us,' said Georgia.

CHAPTER SEVEN

It was dark outside. Georgia and Tim held her arms when they crossed the road. 'What a film!' Tim said.

'I can't believe it's finished,' Joanne said.

'What happened back there?' Georgia said. 'Why did you run into the cinema? Was somebody coming after you?'

'I – I thought they were.'

'*They*?'

'Did anyone follow me into the cinema?' Joanne said.

'We didn't see anyone,' Georgia said.

'Did the town seem quieter than usual tonight?' Joanne asked. 'When I arrived, the streets were empty. The cinema was empty. It was like a story, and I was part of that story. Martin Wisemann will tell you –'

'I *knew* he had something to do with it,' Georgia said.

Joanne tried to think. 'Something important is missing.'

'We must take her home,' Georgia said to Tim.

'How can I make them believe?' Joanne thought. She had lived a story, one of Martin's wildest. Why weren't the monsters dead? Where were they? Something went wrong at the end . . .

'Oh, God!' she said. 'Tim, will you take me to Martin?'

'Why?' Georgia wanted to know. 'What's the matter?'

'He's changed the end of the story,' Joanne said.

◆

'He sent me to my friends, to be safe,' she thought. 'He used the monsters to take me to Georgia and Tim, and then he called them back to himself.'

Tim was driving his father's car. 'Is that the turning to Westbury?' he said.

'Yes,' Georgia said. 'But why is the sky red?'

Fire. Every horror story has its house which burns to the ground with the monster-maker inside. The monsters were inside the burning house, and Martin was with them.

'*This* is the end he wrote,' Joanne thought.

Clouds of smoke were above the house, and burned pages came down from the sky. Thoughts, ideas, stories.

Monsters.

Clouds of smoke were above the cottage, and burned pages came down from the sky. Thoughts, ideas, stories.

♦

Georgia came to Joanne's house the next morning.

'They took a body out of the house this morning,' she said. 'But not the other things you spoke about.'

'Of course not,' Joanne said. 'Martin took *them* with him. They were never real.'

'What are you going to do with your Martin Wisemann books?' Georgia asked.

'I won't keep them,' Joanne said.

And after Georgia went away, Joanne began to take them off the shelves in her room. *Read me*, they seemed to say. *I'm only a story*. But she knew better than that.

There was one she couldn't find – a book of short stories. 'Perhaps it's downstairs,' she thought.

She could hear Jason and Sarah laughing and playing outside in the garden. She went past the door of Sarah's room. The book of short stories was open on Sarah's bed. 'Sarah's reading it,' Joanne thought. She went in and picked it up, and looked at the story on the open page.

Lover Come Back.

Joanne was suddenly cold, and she began to shake. It was quiet outside now. Had Sarah and Jason stopped playing? Then their shouts and screams began again. It was all right. It was nothing to worry about.

Or was it?

She heard feet coming up the stairs, and the book fell from her hand. She saw the dark shape and heard the voice.

'I'm home, dear,' said Billy McGuire.

EXERCISES

Vocabulary Work

Look back at the 'Dictionary Words' in this story. Make sure that you know the meaning of each word.

1 Find Dictionary Words which mean:
   a a place where you put books
   b a place where you sit
   c a sort of food (for breakfast)
   d something you use in supermarkets
   e a room below a house
   f something you can open and close

Write sentences with the words.

2 Write sentences with the words in these groups:
   a grave/cemetery/come alive
   b believe/dream
   c slime/curtains
   d horror/vacuum cleaner

Comprehension

Chapters 1–2

1 Answer these questions:
   a What did the policeman want to know from David?
   b Joanne saw a man in the crowd when the car crashed. Who was he?
   c When was the first time Joanne knew about 'the terrible things monsters could do'?
   d What were most of the 'papers' in Martin Wisemann's room?
   e Why did Joanne run away from Martin Wisemann's house?

Chapters 3–4

2 Who said these things?

 a 'I thought I saw him in two other bookshops this week.'

 b 'You said you loved me, but it was a *lie*.'

 c 'I want to explain things to Billy's parents.'

 d 'So stop feeling sorry for yourself.'

3 Are these sentences true (√) or not true (x)?

 a Billy McGuire is shot dead.

 b *Cereal Killer* is about the Honey Monster.

 c The Honey Monster climbed down a hole in the floor of the supermarket and disappeared.

 d Joanne picked up the little pizzas with the vacuum cleaner.

Chapters 5–7

4 Put these sentences in the right order:

 a She picked it up and shot the THING.

 b 'He's changed the end of the story.'

 c She could see the lights of the town now.

 d A blue-grey slime was over all the grass, and the garden chairs.

 e Joanne pulled herself away from Billy, and Martin took a gun from
 his jacket pocket.

 f At first she saw only darkness, but then she saw grey-white
 shapes.

 g Clouds of smoke were above the house, and burned pages came
 down from the sky.

 h She remembered the gun in the back of the car.

 i The town was empty. The shops were closed.

Discussion

1 Joanne says there *are* monsters, but you don't always realise that's
 what they are at first. Do you agree or disagree with this?

2 Martin Wisemann wrote about the things that he was afraid of. Do you
 think it helps to write about the things that worry you, or frighten you?

Writing

1 Which part of the story do you find the most frightening? Explain why
   in about 100 words.
2 Look at the picture on page 9. Write two or three sentences about the
   people in the picture – their faces, their bodies, their clothes.